SCHOLASTIC

Week-by-Week Homework Packets
Spelling

Grade 3

by Kristin Geller

NEW YORK • TORONTO • LONDON • AUCKLAND • SYDNEY
MEXICO CITY • NEW DELHI • HONG KONG • BUENOS AIRES

Teaching *Resources*

Dedicated to my husband Warren,
for always being my voice of reason and my support system.
Thank you!

Cover design by Lillian Kohli

Interior design by Sydney Wright

ISBN–13: 978-0-439-65098-4

ISBN–10: 0-439-65098-4

Copyright © 2007 by Kristin Geller

Published by Scholastic Inc.

Printed in the U.S.A

4 5 6 7 8 9 10   31   15 14 13 12 11 10

Contents

Spelling Lessons

Introduction

Dear Third-Grade Teacher,

Third grade is a fantastic year! Nothing is more exciting than observing the development of independent students who enjoy reading, writing, and communicating.

One of the greatest challenges that third-grade teachers face is the task of moving their students to the point of independence. Students must become independently proficient in their reading comprehension, writing clarity, and spelling accuracy in order to succeed in school. That's where *Week-by-Week Homework Packets: Spelling Grade 3* comes in. This effective spelling program can help students of varying abilities develop as writers and readers because it provides them with repeated opportunities to read and write essential vocabulary in a consistent and flexible manner. The weekly spelling lists are based on key spelling patterns and include 240 words that students will encounter with greatest frequency in their reading and writing during third grade. This program is mapped out from the beginning to the end of the school year and offers opportunities to differentiate each child's word list to ensure that the needs of all learners are met.

Plus, *Week-by-Week Homework Packets: Spelling Grade 3* is a snap to use. Simply copy three pages for every lesson—an assignment checklist and two pages of spelling activities—to send home with students every Monday. Then, review the words in your classroom throughout the week. (See About This Book on pages 5–7 to find complete how-to's, management tips, and activity ideas.) On Friday, collect the homework and follow with a copy of Spell Check, the student assessment on page 10. Your students will be on their way to successful, independent reading and writing before you know it!

Enjoy—and here's to super spellers!

Sincerely,

Kristin Geller

About This Book

Week-by-Week Homework Packets: Spelling Grade 3 includes 36 weeks of word lists and activities for use throughout the school year. See below for a close-up look at the program's components as well as ideas to help you get the most out of this valuable resource.

Weekly Spelling Lesson Program Components

Weekly Spelling Lesson Packets

The weekly homework packets (pages 12–72) consist of the following three pages:

1. The Weekly Spelling Work Checklist (page 12) lists the homework to be completed each night of the week and asks for a parent signature.

2. The first page of each packet includes an alphabetical ordering activity, and a sentence-writing activity.

3. The second page includes a continuation of the sentence-writing activity, a spelling-pattern activity, and a bonus section.

Simply copy each page, staple together to form a packet, and distribute to students every week to take home and complete.

Weekly Spell Check Assessments

Conduct a Spell Check, the student assessment on page 10 at the end of a week-long study of a word list to assess each student's mastery. This assessment should be administered in a simple, stress-free way that will allow students to demonstrate their competency. After grading, record the information on the Teacher Spell Check Assessment grid (page 11) to track each student's progress. The information you gain from these assessments will help target your differentiation of each child's weekly word list.

Review Lesson Packets

Review Lessons A–F (pages 73–80) will provide students with further practice spelling all 30 words introduced over a five-week period. Review Lesson A includes words from Lessons 1 through 5, Review Lesson B includes words from Lessons 6 through 10, and so on. (See page 9 for a list of all 240 spelling words.) The review lessons consist of the following three pages:

1. The Review Spelling Work Checklist (page 73) lists the homework to be completed each night of the week and asks for a parent signature.

2. The first page of each review packet (pages 74-79) includes a word search, a word scramble, and a review word list.

3. The second page (page 80) includes a sentence-writing activity.

Simply copy each page, staple together to form a packet, and distribute to students during a review week to take home and complete. (The review lessons are not intended to be followed by a Spell Check assessment.)

> ## Home-School Connection
>
> ### Start of the School Year
>
> Involving family members is a wonderful way to incorporate the spelling packets into your classroom and your students' lives. At the start of school, send home a copy of the Family Letter (page 8) which explains the program and describes the expectations for the year. Consider also sending home a copy of the weekly Spell Check, the student assessment on page 10 to give families an idea of the manner in which students will be assessed.

Introducing the Spelling Words

As new spelling words are introduced each week, take the time to discuss the spelling pattern(s) represented by each group of words. For example, while using the homework packet that contains Lesson 4 (page 19) which focuses on long-*o* patterns, review the spelling patterns introduced that create the long-*o* sound: *-o_e* (often referred to as the silent-*e* rule), *-oa*, and *-ow*. Then, if appropriate, add the new list of spelling words to your classroom word wall or word bank. It is important for students to have an introduction to each list of words before working on the homework packet.

Tips for Management & Differentiated Learning

There are a variety of ways to manage this spelling program in your classroom. I've found that using folders or binders is an effective way to organize each child's work. Every week, provide students with a copy of the spelling words to add to their folders/binders. Soon they will have a handy resource of words that they can reference when working on writing tasks! These folders/binders can be kept within each student's desk or in a private work area. Because all students will be working off of the same basic word list, a consistent program is established— but there is also flexibility. The Class Words and My Words sections of the word list present opportunities for differentiation.

- Class Words provide the opportunity to incorporate words from other areas of your curriculum. For example, if your class is studying the rain forest, words such as *canopy*, *endangered*, and *kapok* might be included here.

- My Words provide the opportunity to reinforce or enrich individual word lists. Students who are ready for increased difficulty can add challenging words to this section, while those who require further reinforcement can include troublesome words until mastered. For example, if a student spells *laugh* incorrectly on a Spell Check, he or she can add it to this section the following week.

Extending Learning

Integrate the weekly word lists throughout the school day. Suggestions follow.

Learning Centers

- Word Work Center—Students can complete activities such as stamping the words with letter stamps, writing the words on write-on/wipe-off boards, building the words with magnetic letters and boards, or using the words to write short stories.

- Game Center—Students can play games with the words such as BINGO, Spelling Word Match (similar to the card game Concentration), and Word War (similar to the card game War). Each of these activities requires the creation of game boards and/or word cards, but are well worth the effort.

Morning Message

A wonderful way to start each day is to write a morning message that incorporates both the weekly spelling words and a shared writing activity. During this interactive writing exercise students can circle or highlight spelling words, fill in missing letters, words, and/or phrases, and correct mistakes, all while learning the important skills of sentence structure, grammar, and comprehension.

Fanta_tic morn_ _ _! Today is _riday, _ovem _ _r _ _, _ _ _ _.

Ye_ _erDay, I re_ _ _ _ _D a leTter from a f_ _ _ _ _ of mIne.

In tHe le_ _er she said t_at she w_ _l ta_e a tr_p to t_e state of _laska

to par_icipa_e in a sl_ _ _ _ race. s_e be_ _ _ _ _s that she can actually win!

(This sample message contains some of the spelling words from Lesson 8 on page 27—*field, friend, thief, receive, sleigh, receipt, vein, believe.*)

Dictation Journal

To provide students with opportunities to use spelling words in meaningful ways, and to help assess their understanding, consider using dictation journals with your class. These are used on a weekly basis and can be created with any journal or notebook, or by stapling blank sheets of paper together to form a journal. Begin by dictating a sentence that contains a spelling word. For example, while using the homework packet that contains Lesson 12 (page 35) you might dictate the following sentence: *Last Thursday was my birthday and I ate a thick slice of cake.* Then ask students to underline the spelling word (*thick*). After dictating seven more sentences—one for each of the remaining spelling words—review the sentences as a class to correct for spelling and grammar. The journals can also be used for students to create lists of words that follow the same spelling pattern(s) as their spelling words. And students especially love when a timer is set to create a word list race!

Dear Family,

Your child has spent the last few years in school mastering language—reading, writing, speaking, listening, and spelling. Teachers have spent many hours preparing your child to become an independent learner, and your child has spent many hours practicing the strategies and techniques to become an independent and successful reader, writer, speaker, listener, and speller. Third grade is an important milestone because it further promotes, and then expects, independence and proficiency among these tasks. Your child's spelling words are important words that will reinforce key spelling patterns that all third graders need to know.

Each week your child will bring home a packet that includes a list of spelling words and homework activities. The words and activities will be introduced and reviewed in class, but your child may need further assistance learning to spell the words and completing the activities. The homework packet is due each Friday and will be followed by a Spell Check to assess your child's mastery of the week's words.

You will notice that your child may have additional words in the Class Words or My Words sections of the word list. Class Words are words that we are studying or focusing on as part of a unit of study in our classroom. My Words are words used to differentiate spelling instruction for every student. They are words used to reinforce or enrich your child's individual spelling program.

Thank you for your support in building super spellers!

Sincerely,

Week-by-Week Homework Packets: Spelling Grade 3 Scholastic Teaching Resources

Spelling Lesson Sequence

Lesson 1 (long *a*): brave, face, name, rage, wait, chain, sail, nail
Lesson 2 (long *e*): leave, shield, piece, scream, steep, brief, feed, grief
Lesson 3 (long *i*): high, mine, sigh, fight, wise, mile, tight, time
Lesson 4 (long *o*): spoke, boat, code, soak, hold, float, flow, window
Lesson 5 (long *u*): clue, rude, cute, menu, unit, use, human, fuse
Review Lesson A

Lesson 6 (*oo*): good, cook, look, noon, shoot, stood, hoop, mood
Lesson 7 (*ou/ow*): count, loud, round, allow, town, howl, south, frown
Lesson 8 (*ie/ei*): field, friend, thief, receive, sleigh, receipt, vein, believe
Lesson 9 (*r* blends): brick, treat, bread, grade, true, great, group, trace
Lesson 10 (*l* blends): blend, flag, club, flew, blink, closet, floor, clown
Review Lesson B

Lesson 11 (*s* blends): skill, skirt, stone, smell, step, spring, snake, snack
Lesson 12 (digraphs): church, chance, sheet, shout, while, where, thick, thing
Lesson 13 (digraphs): beach, bunch, crash, bench, watch, fetch, brush, match
Lesson 14 (*ph/gh*): graph, phone, photo, elephant, cough, laugh, rough, tough
Lesson 15 (*/z/*): cheese, please, tease, rise, freeze, prize, quiz, rose
Review Lesson C

Lesson 16 (silent letters): knew, knock, knot, climb, crumb, lamb, wrist, write
Lesson 17 (*dge/ge*): hedge, judge, bridge, large, plunge, edge, sponge, ridge
Lesson 18 (soft c): center, circle, fence, place, price, excite, lace, trace
Lesson 19 (*-es* plurals): dishes, lunches, boxes, washes, teaches, foxes, wishes, inches
Lesson 20 (*-ies* plurals): babies, flies, stories, families, diaries, berries, cries, cities
Review Lesson D

Lesson 21 (*-le*): apple, cable, middle, huddle, table, title, candle, battle
Lesson 22 (*-el*): shovel, cancel, hotel, label, towel, nickel, vowel, channel
Lesson 23 (verb + *-ed*): asked, jumped, walked, cooked, talked, looked, bumped, lasted
Lesson 24 (verb, doubled consonant, + *-ed*): grabbed, hugged, stirred, shopped, tripped, hopped, skipped, stabbed
Lesson 25 (*y* to *i* + *-ed*): carried, tried, cried, studied, fried, flurried, worried, married
Review Lesson E

Lesson 26 (verb + *-ing*): talking, going, reading, singing, hearing, mixing, seeing, feeling
Lesson 27 (verb, doubled consonant, + *-ing*): letting, sitting, mopping, running, cutting, betting, rubbing, swimming
Lesson 28 (verb, drop e, + *-ed/-ing*): danced, skated, wasted, chasing, hoping, writing, tracing, using
Lesson 29 (prefixes): reread, undone, disagree, disorder, rewrite, unfair, disobey, unlock
Lesson 30 (suffixes): careful, sleepless, darkness, useful, hopeless, kindness, hopeful, endless
Review Lesson F

Name _____   Lesson _____

Date _____

Spell Check

1. _____

2. _____

3. _____

4. _____

5. _____

6. _____

7. _____

8. _____

9. _____

10. _____

My Spell Check Score: ☐

10

Week-by-Week Homework Packets: Spelling Grade 3   Scholastic Teaching Resources   Student Spell Check Assessment

Teacher Spell Check Assessment

Teacher _____

Grade _____ Year _____

Student	Lesson 1	Lesson 2	Lesson 3	Lesson 4	Lesson 5	Lesson 6	Lesson 7	Lesson 8	Lesson 9	Lesson 10	Lesson 11	Lesson 12	Lesson 13	Lesson 14	Lesson 15	Lesson 16	Lesson 17	Lesson 18	Lesson 19	Lesson 20	Lesson 21	Lesson 22	Lesson 23	Lesson 24	Lesson 25	Lesson 26	Lesson 27	Lesson 28	Lesson 29	Lesson 30

Name _____

WEEKLY
Spelling Work

☐ **Monday**   ABC Order: Write your words in alphabetical order.

☐ **Tuesday**   Sentences: Write four sentences. Use at least one of your words in each sentence and underline the word(s).

☐ **Wednesday** Sentences: Write four sentences using your remaining words. Use at least one word in each sentence and underline the word(s).

☐ **Thursday**   Spelling Pattern: List other words that follow the same spelling pattern(s) as your spelling words.

☐ **Friday**   Return this homework and be ready for Spell Check!

Parent Signature _____

☐ **BONUS**    Write a short story or a letter to a person of your choice. Include at least five of your words and underline each word. Be creative!

Week-by-Week Homework Packets: Spelling Grade 3 Scholastic Teaching Resources

Name _____

Spelling Words

brave	wait
face	chain
name	sail
rage	nail

Class Words

My Words

ABC Order

1. _____
2. _____
3. _____
4. _____
5. _____
6. _____
7. _____
8. _____
9. _____
10. _____

Sentences

1. _____
   _____
   _____

2. _____
   _____
   _____

3. _____
   _____

4. _____
   _____
   _____

Sentences

5. _____

_____

6. _____

_____

7. _____

_____

8. _____

_____

Spelling Pattern

1. (-a__e) _____   4. (-ai) _____

2. (-a__e) _____   5. (-ai) _____

3. (-a__e) _____   6. (-ai) _____

Bonus

_____

_____

_____

_____

_____

_____

Week-by-Week Homework Packets: Spelling Grade 3 Scholastic Teaching Resources

Name _____

Spelling Words

leave	steep
shield	brief
piece	feed
scream	grief

Class Words

My Words

ABC Order

1. _____
2. _____
3. _____
4. _____
5. _____
6. _____
7. _____
8. _____
9. _____
10. _____

Sentences

1. _____
_____
_____

2. _____
_____
_____

3. _____
_____
_____

4. _____
_____
_____

Sentences

5. _____

_____

6. _____

_____

7. _____

_____

8. _____

_____

Spelling Pattern

1. (-ea) _____   4. (-ee) _____

2. (-ea) _____   5. (-ie) _____

3. (-ee) _____   6. (-ie) _____

Bonus

_____

_____

_____

_____

_____

_____

Week-by-Week Homework Packets: Spelling Grade 3 Scholastic Teaching Resources

Name _____

Spelling Words

high	wise
mine	mile
sigh	tight
fight	time

Class Words

My Words

ABC Order

1. _____
2. _____
3. _____
4. _____
5. _____
6. _____
7. _____
8. _____
9. _____
10. _____

Sentences

1. _____
_____
_____

2. _____
_____
_____

3. _____
_____
_____

4. _____
_____
_____

Sentences

5. _____

_____

6. _____

_____

7. _____

_____

8. _____

_____

Spelling Pattern

1. (-i__e) _____

2. (-i__e) _____

3. (-i__e) _____

4. (-igh) _____

5. (-igh) _____

6. (-igh) _____

Bonus

_____

_____

_____

_____

_____

_____

Week-by-Week Homework Packets: Spelling Grade 3 Scholastic Teaching Resources

Name _____

Spelling Words		Class Words	My Words
spoke	hold		
boat	float		
code	flow		
soak	window		

🅰🅱🅲 Order

1. _____
2. _____
3. _____
4. _____
5. _____
6. _____
7. _____
8. _____
9. _____
10. _____

Sentences

1. _____
_____
_____

2. _____
_____
_____

3. _____
_____
_____

4. _____
_____
_____

Sentences

5. _____

_____

6. _____

_____

7. _____

_____

8. _____

_____

Spelling Pattern

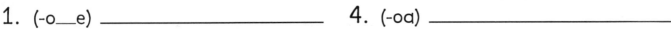

1. (-o__e) _____ 4. (-oa) _____

2. (-o__e) _____ 5. (-ow) _____

3. (-oa) _____ 6. (-ow) _____

Bonus

_____

_____

_____

_____

_____

_____

Week-by-Week Homework Packets: Spelling Grade 3 Scholastic Teaching Resources

Name _____

Spelling Words		**Class Words**	**My Words**
clue	unit		
rude	use		
cute	human		
menu	fuse		

A B C Order

1. _____
2. _____
3. _____
4. _____
5. _____
6. _____
7. _____
8. _____
9. _____
10. _____

Sentences

1. _____
   _____
   _____
2. _____
   _____
   _____
3. _____
   _____
   _____
4. _____
   _____
   _____

Sentences

5. _____

_____

6. _____

_____

7. _____

_____

8. _____

_____

Spelling Pattern

1. (-u__e) _____
2. (-u__e) _____
3. (-ue) _____

4. (-ue) _____
5. (-u) _____
6. (-u) _____

Bonus

_____

_____

_____

_____

_____

_____

Name _____

Spelling Words

good	shoot
cook	stood
look	hoop
noon	mood

Class Words

My Words

ABC Order

1. _____
2. _____
3. _____
4. _____
5. _____
6. _____
7. _____
8. _____
9. _____
10. _____

Sentences

1. _____
_____
_____

2. _____
_____
_____

3. _____
_____
_____

4. _____
_____
_____

Sentences

5. _____

_____

6. _____

_____

7. _____

_____

8. _____

_____

Spelling Pattern

1. (-oo) _____   4. (-oo) _____

2. (-oo) _____   5. (-oo) _____

3. (-oo) _____   6. (-oo) _____

Bonus

_____

_____

_____

_____

_____

_____

Week-by-Week Homework Packets: Spelling Grade 3 Scholastic Teaching Resources

Name _____

Spelling Words

count   town
loud   howl
round   south
allow   frown

Class Words

My Words

ABC Order

1. _____
2. _____
3. _____
4. _____
5. _____
6. _____
7. _____
8. _____
9. _____
10. _____

Sentences

1. _____
   _____
   _____
2. _____
   _____
   _____
3. _____
   _____
   _____
4. _____
   _____
   _____

Sentences

5. _____

_____

6. _____

_____

7. _____

_____

8. _____

_____

Spelling Pattern

1. (-ou) _____   4. (-ow) _____

2. (-ou) _____   5. (-ow) _____

3. (-ou) _____   6. (-ow) _____

Bonus

_____

_____

_____

_____

_____

_____

Week-by-Week Homework Packets: Spelling Grade 3 Scholastic Teaching Resources

Name _____

Spelling Words

field   sleigh
friend   receipt
thief   vein
receive   believe

Class Words

My Words

A B C Order

1. _____
2. _____
3. _____
4. _____
5. _____
6. _____
7. _____
8. _____
9. _____
10. _____

Sentences

1. _____
_____
_____

2. _____
_____
_____

3. _____
_____
_____

4. _____
_____
_____

Sentences

5. _____

_____

6. _____

_____

7. _____

_____

8. _____

_____

Spelling Pattern

1. (-ie) _____   4. (-ei) _____

2. (-ie) _____   5. (-ei) _____

3. (-ie) _____   6. (-ei) _____

Bonus

_____

_____

_____

_____

_____

_____

Week-by-Week Homework Packets: Spelling Grade 3 Scholastic Teaching Resources

Spelling Words

brick	true
treat	great
bread	group
grade	trace

Class Words

My Words

A B C Order

1. _____
2. _____
3. _____
4. _____
5. _____
6. _____
7. _____
8. _____
9. _____
10. _____

Sentences

1. _____
_____
_____

2. _____
_____
_____

3. _____
_____

4. _____
_____
_____

Sentences

5. _____

_____

6. _____

_____

7. _____

_____

8. _____

_____

Spelling Pattern

1. (br-) _____   4. (gr-) _____

2. (br-) _____   5. (tr-) _____

3. (gr-) _____   6. (tr-) _____

Bonus

_____

_____

_____

_____

_____

_____

Week-by-Week Homework Packets: Spelling Grade 3   Scholastic Teaching Resources

Name _____

Spelling Words

blend	blink
flag	closet
club	floor
flew	clown

Class Words

My Words

A B C Order

1. _____
2. _____
3. _____
4. _____
5. _____
6. _____
7. _____
8. _____
9. _____
10. _____

Sentences

1. _____
_____
_____

2. _____
_____
_____

3. _____
_____
_____

4. _____
_____
_____

Sentences

5. _____

_____

6. _____

_____

7. _____

_____

8. _____

_____

Spelling Pattern

1. (bl-) _____   4. (cl-) _____

2. (bl-) _____   5. (fl-) _____

3. (cl-) _____   6. (fl-) _____

Bonus

_____

_____

_____

_____

_____

_____

Week-by-Week Homework Packets: Spelling Grade 3 Scholastic Teaching Resources

Name _____

Spelling Words

skill	step
stone	spring
smell	snake
skirt	snack

Class Words

My Words

A B C Order

1. _____
2. _____
3. _____
4. _____
5. _____
6. _____
7. _____
8. _____
9. _____
10. _____

Sentences

1. _____
   _____
   _____
2. _____
   _____
   _____
3. _____
   _____
   _____
4. _____
   _____
   _____

Sentences

5. _____

_____

6. _____

_____

7. _____

_____

8. _____

_____

Spelling Pattern

1. (sk-) _____   4. (st-) _____

2. (sm-) _____   5. (sp-) _____

3. (sm-) _____   6. (sn-) _____

Bonus

_____

_____

_____

_____

_____

_____

Week-by-Week Homework Packets: Spelling Grade 3 Scholastic Teaching Resources

Name _____

Spelling Words

church	where
sheet	thick
while	shout
chance	thing

Class Words

My Words

ABC Order

1. _____
2. _____
3. _____
4. _____
5. _____
6. _____
7. _____
8. _____
9. _____
10. _____

Sentences

1. _____
_____
_____

2. _____
_____
_____

3. _____
_____
_____

4. _____
_____
_____

Sentences

5. _____

_____

6. _____

_____

7. _____

_____

8. _____

_____

Spelling Pattern

1. (ch-) _____

2. (ch-) _____

3. (sh-) _____

4. (sh-) _____

5. (th-) _____

6. (wh-) _____

Bonus

_____

_____

_____

_____

_____

_____

Week-by-Week Homework Packets: Spelling Grade 3 Scholastic Teaching Resources

Name _____

Spelling Words		Class Words	My Words
beach	bunch		
crash	fetch		
watch	match		
brush	bench		

ABC Order

1. _____

2. _____

3. _____

4. _____

5. _____

6. _____

7. _____

8. _____

9. _____

10. _____

Sentences

1. _____

_____

_____

2. _____

_____

_____

3. _____

_____

_____

4. _____

_____

_____

Sentences

5. _____

_____

6. _____

_____

7. _____

_____

8. _____

_____

Spelling Pattern

1. (-ch) _____

2. (-ch) _____

3. (-ch) _____

4. (-sh) _____

5. (-sh) _____

6. (-sh) _____

Bonus

_____

_____

_____

_____

_____

_____

Week-by-Week Homework Packets: Spelling Grade 3 Scholastic Teaching Resources

Spelling Words

graph   cough
phone   laugh
photo   rough
elephant   tough

Class Words

My Words

AB**C** Order

1. _____
2. _____
3. _____
4. _____
5. _____
6. _____
7. _____
8. _____
9. _____
10. _____

Sentences

1. _____
   _____
   _____
2. _____
   _____
   _____
3. _____
   _____
   _____
4. _____
   _____
   _____

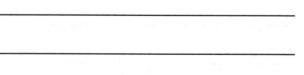

Sentences

5. _____

_____

6. _____

_____

7. _____

_____

8. _____

_____

Spelling Pattern

1. (ph) _____   4. (ph) _____

2. (ph) _____   5. (gh) _____

3. (ph) _____   6. (gh) _____

Bonus

_____

_____

_____

_____

_____

_____

Week-by-Week Homework Packets: Spelling Grade 3 Scholastic Teaching Resources

Name _____

Spelling Words

cheese	freeze
please	prize
tease	quiz
rise	rose

Class Words

My Words

A B C Order

1. _____
2. _____
3. _____
4. _____
5. _____
6. _____
7. _____
8. _____
9. _____
10. _____

Sentences

1. _____

   _____

   _____

2. _____

   _____

   _____

3. _____

   _____

   _____

4. _____

   _____

   _____

Sentences

5. _____

_____

6. _____

_____

7. _____

_____

8. _____

_____

Spelling Pattern

1. (-ze) _____   4. (-ose) _____

2. (-ze) _____   5. (-ees) _____

3. (-ose) _____   6. (-ees) _____

Bonus

_____

_____

_____

_____

_____

_____

Week-by-Week Homework Packets: Spelling Grade 3 Scholastic Teaching Resources

Name _____

Spelling Words

knew	knot
knock	crumb
climb	wrist
lamb	write

Class Words

My Words

A B C Order

1. _____
2. _____
3. _____
4. _____
5. _____
6. _____
7. _____
8. _____
9. _____
10. _____

Sentences

1. _____
_____
_____

2. _____
_____
_____

3. _____
_____

4. _____
_____
_____

Sentences

5. _____

_____

6. _____

_____

7. _____

_____

8. _____

_____

Spelling Pattern

1. (kn-) _____   4. (wr-) _____

2. (kn-) _____   5. (-mb) _____

3. (wr-) _____   6. (-mb) _____

Bonus

_____

_____

_____

_____

_____

_____

Week-by-Week Homework Packets: Spelling Grade 3 Scholastic Teaching Resources

Spelling Words

hedge	plunge
judge	edge
bridge	sponge
large	ridge

Class Words

My Words

ABC Order

1. _____
2. _____
3. _____
4. _____
5. _____
6. _____
7. _____
8. _____
9. _____
10. _____

Sentences

1. _____
_____
_____

2. _____
_____
_____

3. _____
_____
_____

4. _____
_____
_____

Sentences

5. _____

_____

6. _____

_____

7. _____

_____

8. _____

_____

Spelling Pattern

1. (-dge) _____   4. (-dge) _____

2. (-dge) _____   5. (-ge) _____

3. (-dge) _____   6. (-ge) _____

Bonus

_____

_____

_____

_____

_____

_____

Name _____

Spelling Words | Class Words | My Words

Spelling Words		Class Words	My Words
center	price		
fence	excite		
place	lace		
circle	trace		

ABC Order

1. _____
2. _____
3. _____
4. _____
5. _____
6. _____
7. _____
8. _____
9. _____
10. _____

Sentences

1. _____
_____
_____

2. _____
_____
_____

3. _____
_____
_____

4. _____
_____
_____

Sentences

5. _____

_____

6. _____

_____

7. _____

_____

8. _____

_____

Spelling Pattern

1. (c-) _____   4. (-ce) _____

2. (c-) _____   5. (-ce) _____

3. (c-) _____   6. (-ce) _____

Bonus

_____

_____

_____

_____

_____

_____

Week-by-Week Homework Packets: Spelling Grade 3 Scholastic Teaching Resources

Name _____

Spelling Words

dishes	teaches
lunches	foxes
boxes	wishes
washes	inches

Class Words

My Words

A B C Order

1. _____

2. _____

3. _____

4. _____

5. _____

6. _____

7. _____

8. _____

9. _____

10. _____

Sentences

1. _____
   _____
   _____

2. _____
   _____
   _____

3. _____
   _____
   _____

4. _____
   _____
   _____

Sentences

5. _____

_____

6. _____

_____

7. _____

_____

8. _____

_____

Spelling Pattern

1. (-es) _____   4. (-es) _____

2. (-es) _____   5. (-es) _____

3. (-es) _____   6. (-es) _____

Bonus

_____

_____

_____

_____

_____

_____

Week-by-Week Homework Packets: Spelling Grade 3 Scholastic Teaching Resources

Name _____

Spelling Words

babies	diaries
flies	berries
stories	cries
families	cities

Class Words

My Words

AB**C** Order

1. _____
2. _____
3. _____
4. _____
5. _____
6. _____
7. _____
8. _____
9. _____
10. _____

Sentences

1. _____
_____
_____

2. _____
_____
_____

3. _____
_____

4. _____
_____
_____

Sentences

5. _____

_____

6. _____

_____

7. _____

_____

8. _____

_____

Spelling Pattern

1. (-ies) _____   4. (-ies) _____

2. (-ies) _____   5. (-ies) _____

3. (-ies) _____   6. (-ies) _____

Bonus

_____

_____

_____

_____

_____

_____

Week-by-Week Homework Packets: Spelling Grade 3 Scholastic Teaching Resources

Name _____

Spelling Words | Class Words | My Words

apple   table

cable   title

middle   candle

huddle   battle

ABC Order

1. _____

2. _____

3. _____

4. _____

5. _____

6. _____

7. _____

8. _____

9. _____

10. _____

Sentences

1. _____

_____

_____

2. _____

_____

_____

3. _____

_____

_____

4. _____

_____

_____

Sentences

5. _____

_____

6. _____

_____

7. _____

_____

8. _____

_____

Spelling Pattern

1. (-le) _____   4. (-le) _____

2. (-le) _____   5. (-le) _____

3. (-le) _____   6. (-le) _____

Bonus

_____

_____

_____

_____

_____

_____

Week-by-Week Homework Packets: Spelling Grade 3 Scholastic Teaching Resources

Name _____

Spelling Words

shovel   towel

cancel   nickel

hotel   vowel

label   channel

Class Words

My Words

ⒶⒷⒸ Order

1. _____

2. _____

3. _____

4. _____

5. _____

6. _____

7. _____

8. _____

9. _____

10. _____

Sentences

1. _____
_____
_____

2. _____
_____
_____

3. _____
_____
_____

4. _____
_____
_____

Sentences

5. _____

_____

6. _____

_____

7. _____

_____

8. _____

_____

Spelling Pattern

1. (-el) _____   4. (-el) _____

2. (-el) _____   5. (-el) _____

3. (-el) _____   6. (-el) _____

Bonus

_____

_____

_____

_____

_____

_____

Week-by-Week Homework Packets: Spelling Grade 3 Scholastic Teaching Resources

Spelling Words

asked	talked
jumped	looked
walked	bumped
cooked	lasted

Class Words

My Words

⬛A⬛B⬛C Order ✦

1. _____

2. _____

3. _____

4. _____

5. _____

6. _____

7. _____

8. _____

9. _____

10. _____

Sentences ✦

1. _____
_____
_____

2. _____
_____
_____

3. _____
_____
_____

4. _____
_____
_____

Sentences

5. _____

_____

6. _____

_____

7. _____

_____

8. _____

_____

Spelling Pattern

1. (-ed) _____   4. (-ed) _____

2. (-ed) _____   5. (-ed) _____

3. (-ed) _____   6. (-ed) _____

Bonus

_____

_____

_____

_____

_____

_____

Week-by-Week Homework Packets: Spelling Grade 3 Scholastic Teaching Resources

Spelling Words

grabbed	tripped
hugged	hopped
stirred	skipped
shopped	stabbed

Class Words

My Words

A B C Order

1. _____

2. _____

3. _____

4. _____

5. _____

6. _____

7. _____

8. _____

9. _____

10. _____

Sentences

1. _____
_____
_____

2. _____
_____
_____

3. _____
_____

4. _____
_____
_____

Sentences

5. _____

_____

6. _____

_____

7. _____

_____

8. _____

_____

Spelling Pattern

1. -doubled
   consonant (ed) _____

2. -doubled
   consonant (ed) _____

3. -doubled
   consonant (ed) _____

4. -doubled
   consonant (ed) _____

5. -doubled
   consonant (ed) _____

6. -doubled
   consonant (ed) _____

Bonus

_____

_____

_____

_____

_____

_____

Week-by-Week Homework Packets: Spelling Grade 3 Scholastic Teaching Resources

Name _____

Spelling Words

carried	fried
tried	flurried
cried	worried
studied	married

Class Words

My Words

A B C Order

1. _____

2. _____

3. _____

4. _____

5. _____

6. _____

7. _____

8. _____

9. _____

10. _____

Sentences

1. _____
_____
_____

2. _____
_____
_____

3. _____
_____
_____

4. _____
_____
_____

Sentences

5. _____

_____

6. _____

_____

7. _____

_____

8. _____

_____

Spelling Pattern

1. -y to i (ied) _____

2. -y to i (ied) _____

3. -y to i (ied) _____

4. -y to i (ied) _____

5. -y to i (ied) _____

6. -y to i (ied) _____

Bonus

_____

_____

_____

_____

_____

_____

Week-by-Week Homework Packets: Spelling Grade 3 Scholastic Teaching Resources

Spelling Words

talking	hearing
going	mixing
reading	seeing
singing	feeling

Class Words

My Words

ABC Order

1. _____
2. _____
3. _____
4. _____
5. _____
6. _____
7. _____
8. _____
9. _____
10. _____

Sentences

1. _____
_____
_____

2. _____
_____
_____

3. _____
_____
_____

4. _____
_____
_____

Sentences

5. _____

_____

6. _____

_____

7. _____

_____

8. _____

_____

Spelling Pattern

1. (-ing) _____

2. (-ing) _____

3. (-ing) _____

4. (-ing) _____

5. (-ing) _____

6. (-ing) _____

Bonus

_____

_____

_____

_____

_____

_____

_____

Week-by-Week Homework Packets: Spelling Grade 3 Scholastic Teaching Resources

Name _____

Spelling Words

letting	cutting
sitting	betting
mopping	rubbing
running	swimming

Class Words

My Words

A B C Order

1. _____

2. _____

3. _____

4. _____

5. _____

6. _____

7. _____

8. _____

9. _____

10. _____

Sentences

1. _____
_____
_____

2. _____
_____
_____

3. _____
_____
_____

4. _____
_____

Sentences

5. _____

_____

6. _____

_____

7. _____

_____

8. _____

_____

Spelling Pattern

1. -doubled consonant (ing) _____

2. -doubled consonant (ing) _____

3. -doubled consonant (ing) _____

4. -doubled consonant (ing) _____

5. -doubled consonant (ing) _____

6. -doubled consonant (ing) _____

Bonus

_____

_____

_____

_____

_____

_____

Week-by-Week Homework Packets: Spelling Grade 3   Scholastic Teaching Resources

Name _____

Spelling Words

danced   wasted

chasing   hoping

writing   tracing

skated   using

Class Words

My Words

ABC Order

1. _____

2. _____

3. _____

4. _____

5. _____

6. _____

7. _____

8. _____

9. _____

10. _____

Sentences

1. _____

_____

_____

2. _____

_____

_____

3. _____

_____

_____

4. _____

_____

_____

Sentences

5. _____

_____

6. _____

_____

7. _____

_____

8. _____

_____

Spelling Pattern

1. -drop e (ing) _____
2. -drop e (ing) _____
3. -drop e (ing) _____

4. -drop e (ed) _____
5. -drop e (ed) _____
6. -drop e (ed) _____

Bonus

_____

_____

_____

_____

_____

_____

Week-by-Week Homework Packets: Spelling Grade 3 Scholastic Teaching Resources

Name _____

Spelling Words

reread	rewrite
undone	unfair
disagree	disobey
disorder	unlock

Class Words

My Words

ABC Order

1. _____
2. _____
3. _____
4. _____
5. _____
6. _____
7. _____
8. _____
9. _____
10. _____

Sentences

1. _____
_____
_____

2. _____
_____
_____

3. _____
_____
_____

4. _____
_____
_____

Sentences ✦ ✦ ✦ ✦ ✦ ✦ ✦ ✦ ✦ ✦

5. _____

_____

6. _____

_____

7. _____

_____

8. _____

_____

Spelling Pattern ✦ ✦ ✦ ✦ ✦ ✦ ✦ ✦ ✦

1. (re-) _____   4. (un-) _____

2. (re-) _____   5. (dis-) _____

3. (un-) _____   6. (dis-) _____

Bonus ✦ ✦ ✦ ✦ ✦ ✦ ✦ ✦ ✦ ✦

_____

_____

_____

_____

_____

_____

Week-by-Week Homework Packets: Spelling Grade 3 Scholastic Teaching Resources

Name _____

Spelling Words

careful   hopeless

sleepless   kindness

darkness   hopeful

useful   endless

Class Words

My Words

ABC Order

1. _____

2. _____

3. _____

4. _____

5. _____

6. _____

7. _____

8. _____

9. _____

10. _____

Sentences

1. _____

_____

_____

2. _____

_____

_____

3. _____

_____

_____

4. _____

_____

_____

Sentences

5. _____

_____

6. _____

_____

7. _____

_____

8. _____

_____

Spelling Pattern

1. (-ful) _____

2. (-ful) _____

3. (-ness) _____

4. (-ness) _____

5. (-less) _____

6. (-less) _____

Bonus

_____

_____

_____

_____

_____

_____

_____

Week-by-Week Homework Packets: Spelling Grade 3 Scholastic Teaching Resources

Name _____

REVIEW
Spelling Work

☐ **Monday**   Word Search: Find the review words from the word bank in the word search and circle them. Look across and down.

☐ **Tuesday**   Word Scramble: Unscramble the review words to find all the words from the word bank. Write the words correctly on the blank lines.

☐ **Wednesday**   Review Words: Read all of the review words from the list. Ask a family member or friend to listen while you correctly spell each word aloud.

☐ **Thursday**   Sentences: Write five sentences. In each sentence use as many review words as you can. Underline the review word(s) in each sentence.

☐ **Friday**   Return this homework.

Parent Signature _____

Word Search

Word Bank

use	wait
name	nail
feed	leave
grief	window
tight	sigh
hold	rude
soak	time
human	

```
h u m a n l s i g h
j s k n a m e l s r
w e u h i k t i m e
i x y o l e a v e q
n a w l f s o a k r
d c a d i j m z n u
o t i g h t f e e d
w b t d g r i e f e
```

Word Scramble

Word Bank

sail	clue	code	menu	cute
fight	shield	spoke	wise	mine
piece	brave	chain	float	scream

vearb _____

ncahi _____

doec _____

gftih _____

uemn _____

tofla _____

iecpe _____

ecasrm _____

osekp _____

hildes _____

swei _____

lsia _____

inme _____

ectu _____

lecu _____

Review Words

brave	face
name	rage
wait	chain
sail	nail
feed	steep
brief	shield
grief	piece
leave	scream
time	mile
wise	fight
high	tight
sigh	mine
hold	boat
soak	float
spoke	code
flow	window
clue	menu
unit	use
cute	rude
fuse	human

Week-by-Week Homework Packets: Spelling Grade 3 · Scholastic Teaching Resources

Name _____

Word Search

Word Bank

vein	club
hoop	allow
count	shoot
stood	grade
flag	true
howl	field
thief	clown
group	

```
i k e t h i e f z g
y a l l o w z i t r
g c l o w n j e r o
h o o p l x u l u u
v u f c g r a d e p
e n l s h o o t y q
i t a d b w c l u b
n p g f s t o o d e
```

Word Scramble

Word Bank

look	town	cook	mood	frown
trace	round	friend	blink	floor
brick	bread	closet	sleigh	receipt

domo _____   lofor _____

ookc _____   ontw _____

duron _____   etarc _____

wfnro _____   klbin _____

difern _____   okol _____

elsgih _____

ceeptir _____

dbera _____

cirbk _____

lteosc _____

Review Words

good	cook
look	noon
shoot	stood
hoop	mood
count	loud
round	allow
town	howl
south	frown
field	vein
thief	sleigh
friend	receipt
believe	receive
true	brick
treat	bread
grade	great
group	trace
blend	flag
club	flew
blink	closet
floor	clown

Week-by-Week Homework Packets: Spelling Grade 3 Scholastic Teaching Resources

Name _____

Word Search

Word Bank

rise	quiz
smell	thick
prize	bench
graph	beach
step	rose
skirt	shout
photo	match
chance	

```
p h o t o g b c i r
r o s e d r e s b i
j k t c h a n c e s
s m e l l p c n a e
k l p y f h h l c j
i w z i m a t c h s
r q u i z s h o u t
t h i c k p r i z e
```

Word Scramble

Word Bank

skill	laugh	crash	bunch	phone
sheet	watch	please	snack	cough
thing	where	spring	tough	cheese

gipnsr _____

tehes _____

nbcuh _____

gocuh _____

gihnt _____

ehesce _____

hawct _____

gulah _____

seelap _____

ugtoh _____

lklis _____

hreew _____

rhacs _____

neohp _____

caskn _____

Review Words

step	skill
skirt	smell
stone	snake
snack	spring
sheet	shout
while	where
thick	thing
church	chance
crash	beach
bunch	bench
watch	fetch
brush	match
graph	phone
photo	cough
laugh	rough
tough	elephant
rise	quiz
rose	prize
tease	please
cheese	freeze

Week-by-Week Homework Packets: Spelling Grade 3 Scholastic Teaching Resources

Name _____

Word Search

k n o t n p l a c e l
j u d g e l a f e g a
d w s r f x c n n s m
i f l i e s e s t i b
s q a d k q k n e w o
h f r g x y n t r p x
e d g e c f o x e s e
s j e z b e r r i e s

Word Bank

knot	lace
lamb	knew
edge	flies
boxes	center
foxes	place
large	ridge
judge	dishes
berries	

Word Scramble

Word Bank

cries	price	knock	crumb	circle
trace	sponge	families	write	hedge
plunge	wishes	babies	lunches	teaches

knkoc _____   iebbsa _____

dghee _____   npgule _____

eclirc _____   scire _____

icerp _____   eartc _____

bcmru _____   iertw _____

unheslc _____

gepsno _____

wsiehs _____

eecahst _____

liimeafs _____

Review Words

knew	knot
lamb	climb
wrist	write
crumb	knock
edge	judge
large	hedge
ridge	plunge
bridge	sponge
lace	trace
place	price
fence	circle
center	excite
dishes	boxes
washes	teaches
foxes	wishes
inches	lunches
flies	cries
cities	babies
stories	families
diaries	berries

Name _____

Word Search

Word Bank

title	tried
cried	asked
table	hotel
label	married
vowel	hopped
skipped	middle
cooked	hugged
talked	

```
l c a m i d d l e i j f e m
c w s q s z t a l k e d s a
o c k i f t a b l e k b h r
o r e j h d k e p y l c o r
k i d v o w e l o w r s p i
e e p m t r i e d z e t p e
d d v n e b c g h u g g e d
o t i t l e s k i p p e d e
```

Word Scramble

Word Bank

apple	table	towel	cable	cancel
nickel	walked	tripped	carried	studied
looked	jumped	stirred	grabbed	worried

elcba _____   plpae _____

cclaen _____   icekln _____

pjdmue _____   kloedo _____

tsrirde _____   lewot _____

ledkaw _____   laetb _____

rdricea _____

dsteiud _____

iptrepd _____

bgbrdae _____

rwideor _____

Review Words

title	table
apple	cable
battle	huddle
candle	middle
hotel	label
towel	nickel
vowel	shovel
cancel	channel
asked	walked
cooked	talked
looked	bumped
lasted	jumped
grabbed	hugged
stirred	shopped
tripped	hopped
skipped	stabbed
carried	tried
cried	studied
fried	flurried
worried	married

Week-by-Week Homework Packets: Spelling Grade 3 Scholastic Teaching Resources

Name _____

Word Search

Word Bank

using	going
sitting	reread
undone	mixing
tracing	writing
careful	endless
danced	hopeful
rewrite	letting
singing	

```
s d v t r a c i n g c h i
i a p o e y x f k u s o l
n n u z w r i t i n g p e
g c r e r e a d h d o e t
i e j m i x i n g o i f t
n d s i t t i n g n n u i
g c a r e f u l a e g l n
u s i n g e n d l e s s g
```

Word Scramble

Word Bank

reading	kindness	talking	chasing	running
mopping	seeing	cutting	skated	disagree
wasted	unlock	unfair	useful	hopeless

dteasw _____

lsfueu _____

dgerani _____

gnuninr _____

eiadgers _____

pimgonp _____

kaltgin _____

atsekd _____

noculk _____

slsepeoh _____

utcnitg _____

skdinsne _____

negise _____

higancs _____

rfuani _____

Review Words

talking	going
reading	singing
hearing	mixing
seeing	feeling
letting	sitting
mopping	running
cutting	betting
rubbing	swimming
danced	skated
wasted	chasing
hoping	writing
tracing	using
reread	undone
disagree	disorder
rewrite	unfair
disobey	unlock
useful	endless
hopeful	careful
sleepless	darkness
hopeless	kindness

Sentences

1. _____

_____

_____

2. _____

_____

_____

3. _____

_____

_____

4. _____

_____

_____

5. _____

_____

_____

Week-by-Week Homework Packets: Spelling Grade 3   Scholastic Teaching Resources